Landscapes

Book 7

in

"Quick Tips by a Pro Photographer" Series

by Julia Harwood

Contents

Introduction

To start off Landscapes I am going to recommend you read my book on composition. Composition is something we use in all areas of photography, but we tend to use more of them in Landscape Photography. You can get it here as an e-book https://kdp.amazon.com/bookshelf or here as a paperback https://www.createspace.com/5504586

One of the things I get asked a lot, especially by non-photographers, is what camera and lens I use.

To me it's a bit of a strange question, a bit like asking a painter what brand of brushes they use, or a builder what kind of hammers the use but I suppose it's understandable.

The fact of the matter is the camera

and lenses don't make a huge difference in terms of the end result.

Yes it's true that high-end cameras produce higher resolution images with less noise, expensive lenses give you slightly sharper images etc, but unless you are making huge prints or pixel-peeping then they aren't that important.

When someone says, "wow, you must have a good camera", ask them why?
They will probably say something like, "because it takes great pictures," so gently ask them what makes a good painter, is it his brushes, or what makes a good cook, is it her oven?
Then smile and leave them to ponder.

2. Tools and Gear

A great tool for landscape photographers is "The Photographers Ephemeris." This piece of software will tell you the exact time of sunrise, sunset, moonrise, and moonset at any given date for any location in the world. Not only that but it will also show you the direction that the sun and moon will be at those times. By knowing exactly where the sun will rise or set, you can plan your shots accordingly. You can get it as an app for iphone or android.

Polarisers
Often we are out shooting landscapes when it is not dawn or dusk, particularly if we are traveling, so a polariser is a great filter to

have, it darkens the sky,
adds more definition to clouds,
reduces glare and enables you to
shoot through windows or water
much more easily.

ND Filters are another great edition
to your kit, especially if you want to
take long exposure shots like smooth
water, silky waterfalls or moving
clouds.

Tripod

While we are talking about
equipment a tripod and a remote
shutter release are two invaluable
tools. Yes you can find a post to
balance your camera on and you can
use the timer function on your
camera, but these restrict how and
what you can photograph.

I recommend a lightweight but sturdy tripod, these cost a bit more, but maybe suggest it as a family birthday or Christmas present, so other members of the family or fiends can put in to get you a good one.

What is a good tripod?

As I said, lightweight yet sturdy, this is so you will not mind taking it with you and it won't matter if it is a bit windy. Most tripods either have a hook on the center column or if you take the rubber boots off the feet they will have spots you can put a peg through to anchor it. If you have a camera Bag, attaching it to the center pole is sufficient to stabilise the tripod.

I prefer a tripod where the center pole is in two bits a small and a long length or a center pole that is reversible. This allows you to get down very low with your camera, essential for macro work, but great to add foreground interest or to get that unusual angle.

I also like one that has different settings for the legs, so the legs can be very close together, or wide apart as well as something in between.

Make sure you can move the camera smoothly and easily on the tripod in case you want to do video or panoramas. I prefer using one with a trigger or joystick grip that you move camera to the position and then push the button to lock it.

Others prefer ones that have ones that have separate locking for each angle, as in up and down, vertical to horizontal and tilting. So have a play with a few before deciding what is best for you.

Wet weather gear
Always make sure your camera bag has a waterproof cover and you have a plastic bag and a shower cap to protect your camera while still being able to use it. I have a photography cape which is like a poncho with a hood but is big enough for the tripod, camera and me to all fit under.

Using a shower cap I put it over the camera and use an elastic band to secure the opening to the lens barrel and you can do the same with a

plastic bag.
If it is a clear plastic you can still see the controls and the LCD screen.

When organising your gear get a *camera bag* that is easy for you to both carry and access. I use two systems. One is a Lowerpro backpack that swings around when I release one strap and opens from the side so I have access to my gear and it forms a table if I need to balance something on it. The other system is a black adder gear belt and the pouches for my camera, lenses, filters etc.

The advantage of this is it gives quick ready access and you have the weight evenly distributed around you, the disadvantage is it makes you wider so getting through

narrow spaces can be tricky.
However we can also struggle with
narrow ledges with the back pack, so
think about where you are going and
what you might need.

If you look at my second book in the
Quick Tips from a Pro Photographer
called Making Photography Easy it
gives you a list of what you may
want to include in your camera bag.

3. Location

Pick a location that is out of the way of road and foot traffic, where you're unlikely to be disturbed.

Go to the location in broad daylight before the shoot, and ensure your view of the horizon will be unobstructed and the area free of any hazards.

It is always best if you can explore the area in the middle of the day when the light is generally too harsh to take photos. (You can take photos at this time, especially intimate landscapes, but we will cover that further on). Doing this enables you to pre-visualize your shots and get some compositions in mind before the actual shoot.

The last thing you want to be doing when the light is right is desperately trying to find some good compositions.

Obviously if you are traveling through areas and not stopping then you don't have this luxury, but the more you practice it around places you can the easier it will be to know what works and what doesn't, what to look for and what to avoid and so make you a better photographer and able to get those images that you would have missed before.

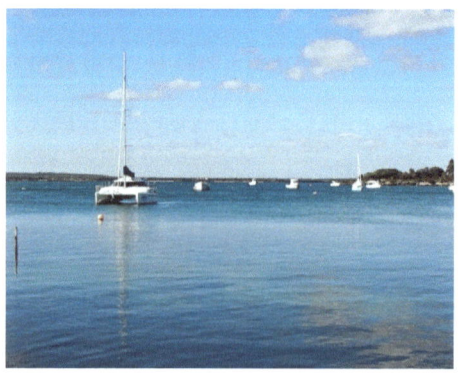

4. What is a Landscape?

There are two views of what a landscape is, one is a traditional view that landscapes are images that show the visual features of an area of land and don't contain human elements. However as the world is becoming more populated there are less and less opportunities to capture these places.

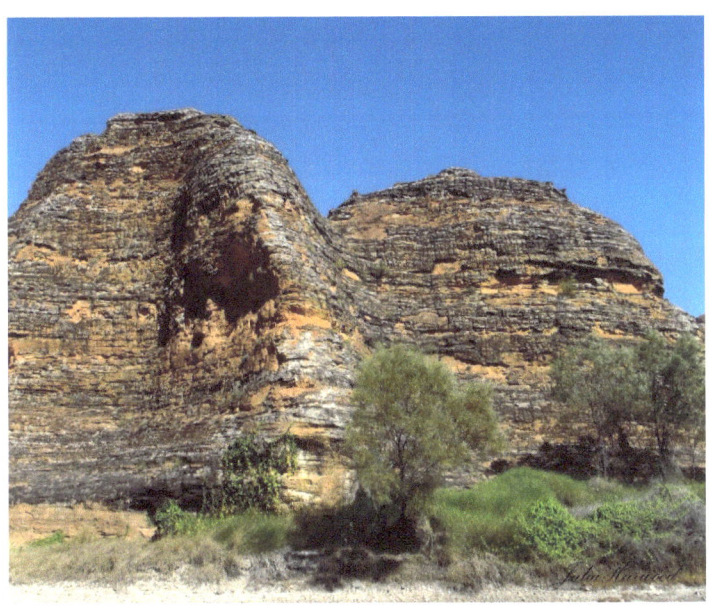

The second views is that a landscape is the visual features of an area overlaid with human elements including land use and buildings. This is what we capture more often.

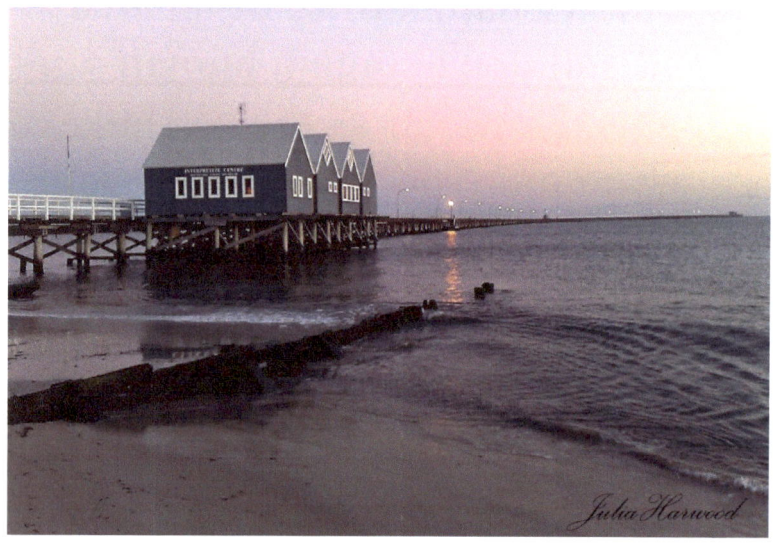

Photography is also often broken up into different elements, so within a category of landscape we have the sub-catagories of sunset/sunrises, waterscapes or seascapes, cityscapes and general landscapes.

There is another one I want you to think about and it is one referred to as 'intimate landscapes'. This is a small area of a landscape that reflects the essence of the landscape and a sense of place and these are often much easier to capture without any human elements.

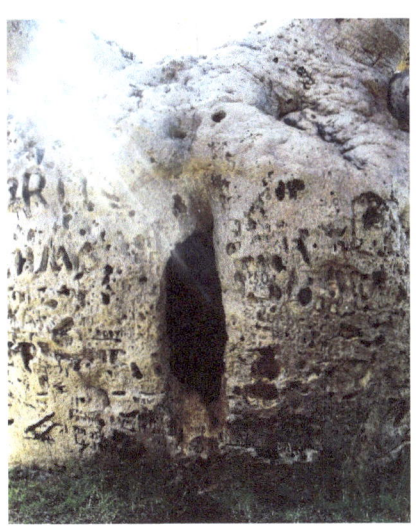

5. Seeing

Seeing is part of composition, but it is also a lot more than that and is something we use in all areas of photography.

It is seeing the scene, interpreting it and capturing a three dimensional image in a two dimensional photograph. This is why people often say it was so much better when we were there, or, the photo doesn't do it justice. This is also where the "art" of photography comes in.

If we shot the scene in 3D it would be just as it was, but in 2D we have to use composition to add the feeling of depth, make sure the contrast is right to show what it was like in 3D.

The first thing we need to look at is light, where is it coming from, is it hard or soft light, does it have a cold, blue tint or a warm gold tint to it?.

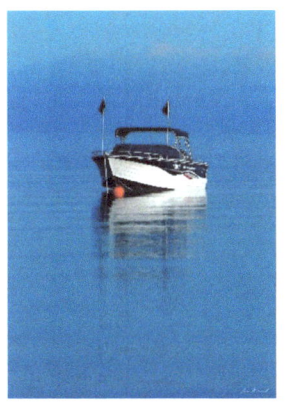 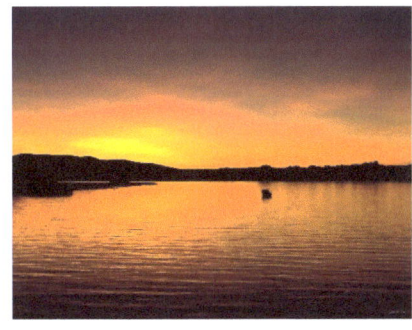

Look at the clouds, what patterns are they creating, how fast are they moving. Clouds are also a key to creating a more 3 dimensional image, so when you see clouds don't despair, instead use them to recreate the feel of the place.

Look for patterns in the sand, sky or landscape.

What direction is the wind coming from?

Look at the water, is it rough, smooth, does it have reflections. Look at shadows, where do they fall, are they hard or soft, long or short, do they fall on other objects in the scene.

Basically we have to start taking the time to really look at what is around us, not just the obvious things, but the subtle things that all go to make up the final image. This will again set you in good stead for all areas of photography.

Remember we are learning to paint with light, which is what photography means.

When we see a landscape that grabs our attention, we tend to stop take a picture and move on. The problem with this is 95% of the time you are going to be disappointed.

Our eyes see in three dimensions but a photo is only 2 dimensional, what this does is flatten the image, so things we see as being separate or in the foreground are going to be smack on top of what is in the background.

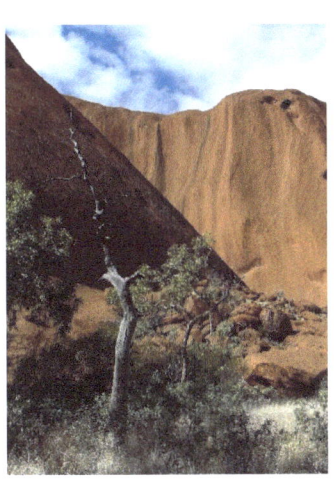

Here are some composition tools
that will help us achieve this.

Leading Lines

There are ways we can create a 3d
feel to a 2D image. A lot of this
comes back to composition, but a
few things that really help in a
landscape image are what we call
leading lines.

We need something to lead our
viewers eyes so they will follow it
and go through the whole scene,
doing this also helps add a sense of
perspective because as the path or
fence or tree line get further away
they will appear smaller.

We can have a strong leading line, like a road or a fence or it can be more of an implied leading line, where shadow meets highlight or where one field ends or another starts, so start looking for leading lines as you wander around.

You will be amazed at how many there are.

Keep an extra eye out for curvy lines as these really make an image intriguing.

Perspective

This is something also that helps the image appear more 3 dimensional.

If we have a known object in the image then we are able to work out how far away it is by it's size.

People, animals, cars, houses and trees all work well.

If we can create a vanishing point by having two leading lines that either come together in the image or imply a vanishing point in the distance, such as a road, this also helps with bringing depth to the image.

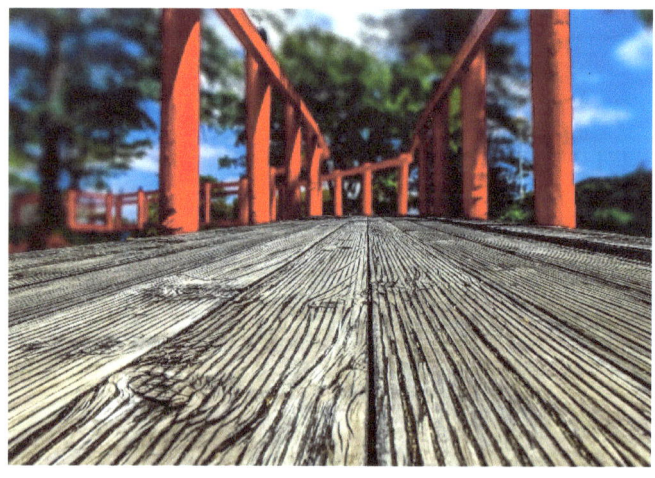

Foreground
Next we look at the foreground elements.

If you can include a foreground element you add an extra layer of interest to the image as well as giving a better perspective and making the viewer feel they are standing right beside you.

You will often have to get low down to get this element, so again start looking for things you can use in a scene.

It could be the weeds, or flowers, a chair, a piece of seaweed, a log, or your own toes.

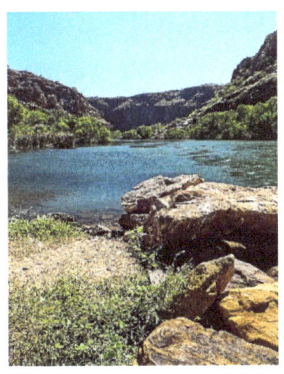

Midground

Again by having a foreground, midground and background we are adding layers which adds a feeling of depth to the image and keeps drawing our attention further in to the image.

Background

This is something people often forget about, if we have a leading line or a disappearing vanishing point, where is it leading us to, if there is nothing we will have an image that feels incomplete and creates a feeling of unease in the viewer, a bit like reading a book and finding the last chapter is missing.

The sky and especially clouds can be a great background.

Cloudy days are great as they give us some soft light, but also they really add an extra dimension to an image.

One thing I recommend when you have clouds in your image is to boost your contrast in post processing as this will usually make them really pop. If the rest of the image doesn't need added contrast, then just select the sky and add it there.

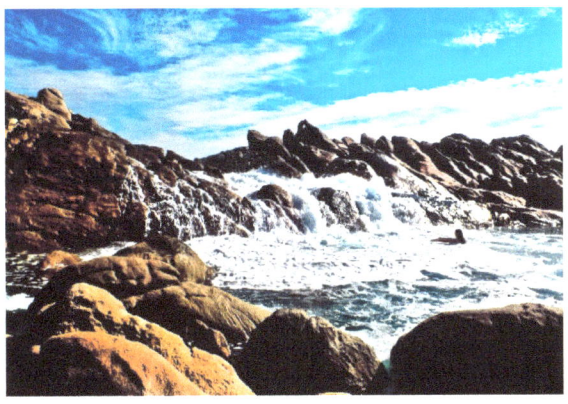

What is your image about?
Another beautiful landscape, a beautiful ocean seascape or a great sunset or sunrise, what will set them apart from the millions of others is if they tell a story.

What made you think I really want to capture this?

Was it the light?

They play of light and shadow?

The colors?

The object within the image?

The sky or the clouds?

Knowing why we are drawn to take an image is important as it gives us a focal point.

The main element that drew us we want to put on one of the intersecting lines of the composition rules or even if we are breaking the rules, we want our focus to be pin sharp on this area.

Balance

We need balance to make an image work. So we have our main object, we know roughly where we want it in the image, are there any lines leading to it, real or implied, if we move around to the left or the right can we find a line?

Is there something we can add to the foreground?

If we do we need it to be smaller than the object we are drawn to so it doesn't overwhelm it.

Is there something in the background we can balance it with?

Can we move to an angle where we create some room between each element like here.

If there is on separation between the objects the scene often just looks busy or confusing,

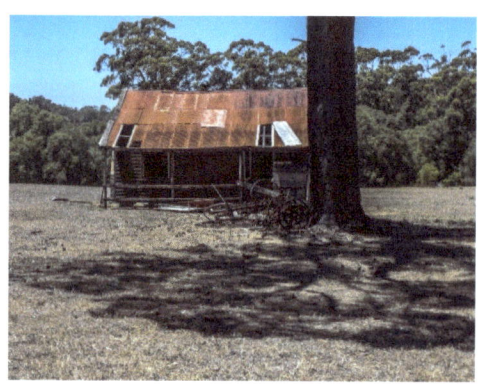

but by moving so that you can see between the object will add to the composition of the image.

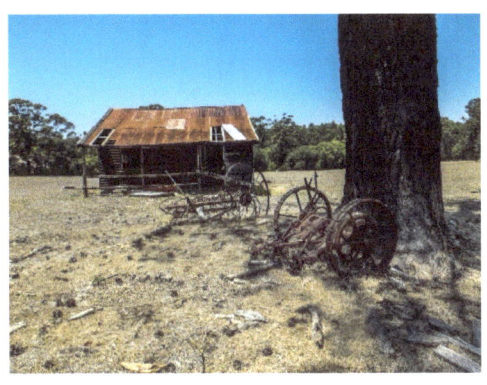

Also while on background, take a moment to scan around your viewfinder, see what is in the image, look at the edges of the frame, is something half in and half out?

Would it look better all in or all out?

Is there any rubbish on the ground, bins in the background or trees growing out of people's heads?

Sometimes we only really see then when we look at the image, so review the image in your LCD screen looking for things that might detract from the image.

Remember to watch out for man made objects like power lines that can detract from an image or a vapor trail when you are trying to portray unspoiled wilderness.

Some of these can be removed in post processing, but the more aware of them you are the more chance you have to look for ways around them.

Color
Now we need to look at color, are there some complimentary colors

that stand out, can we add a pop of red or blue?

Light is always what will ultimately make or break and image, so pay attention to where the light is coming from.

Where do the shadows fall?

Are they hard or soft?

Do they add to the image or distract?

Golden hour and blue hour are said to be the best times to go out and take photos, so they go out early in the morning or later in the afternoon to ensure the best light and this is true, but often we don't have the option.

When we see that landscape we want to capture it is the middle of the day we need to learn what to look out for so that we can still capture a great image.

The reason the golden hour is loved for all photography is because the light has a lovely warm golden tint to it.

For landscapes we usually use a tripod and not a lot of moving objects, so these really lend themselves to the longer shutter speed needed to capture an image in this light.

Blue light is the 20 minutes after the last of the sun set before the sky goes really dark and this is great for images with lights, such as night city scenes or light painting.

I cover sunset and sunrises in detail along with light painting and night photos in my third book, "Low Light Photography".
What do we do if it is the middle of the day and why is that so bad?

The reason midday is said to be worst for photography is that the light is very harsh, the shadows are very strong and colors are often washed out.

But if we add a ND filter we reduce the light and make the colors more saturated.

The same with a polarising filter.

A polarising filter is usually used to make the sky look bluer, to reduce glare and reflections, but for it to be effective you need the sun to be at a 90 degree angle to the front of the lens.
This means the sun should be to your side, not behind or in front of you.

Have a look here for a video on how to use one
https://www.youtube.com/watch?v=0qxrL9SdywM

If it is a cloudy day then the cloud acts as a natural soft-box and softens the light.

If the whole sky is covered with cloud, that is a good time to shoot portraits or flowers unless you don't have any other option.

However if the cloud is allowing some of the sky to shine through, then you have one element of a great scene and you can wait for the sun to move behind a cloud before taking the shot.

During the brighter times of the day is also a great time to shoot 'intimate landscapes', as you can be selective about the scene you use.

An intimate landscape may be a rock with moss growing on it with a flower in the foreground and a little sky in the top corner.

By seeing these mini landscapes, you can walk right around the area and find the best angle or realize that it won't work and move on to find a different area.

I find that often in the middle of the day with no clouds is great to us a polarising filter and take photos of clear water, The clouds are not shadowing the water so you can get great photos like this.

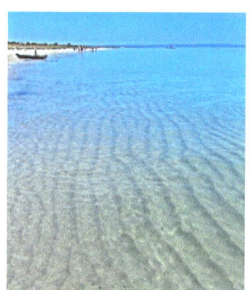

If you are looking to shoot a rainbow, put the sun behind you and face the clouds, rain or water fountain and then you have the best chance of seeing it.

Take a few shots, one exposing for the scene and then one exposing for the rainbow itself.

Remember to keep your camera dry, see my second book on "Making Photography Easy" for more details.

Angles

Also look at different angles, see where the shadows fall, see if you can add them them to the composition.

Depth of field

Generally in Landscape images we want the majority of the image in focus. This means we want a large depth of field or a high f stop such as f11 or more.

The way to achieve the best focus area is known as the hyperfocal distance. Basically this means focusing a third of the way into the image as the focus area falls 1/3 in front of and 2/3 behind the actual focal point.

Sometimes we will choose to use a smaller depth of field to create a certain feeling or mood, so remember these are guidelines, not rules.

White Balance

This is what determines the color in the image. The camera automatically assumes the largest area of a scene will be middle grey and so works the colors out from there however if you have a very white scene like the beach, snow or a wedding then the white areas will appear blue instead of white.

To help the camera we can set the white balance for the type of day, ie cloudy, shade, sunlight etc or we can use a grey card.
This is where you add a piece of grey card to the image and then in post processing you batch all the images white balance to this or better yet if you shoot in RAW you can set the white balance when you process the image.

A final note:

As photographers, as opposed to painters, we start with a canvas that is jam packed, so we have to take objects out to create the image we want. We generally don't have the option of adding elements.

We do this by changing the angle we shoot from to exclude things, or moving things (rubbish), or using a shallower depth of field.

Have fun and enjoy nature.

6. Cheat Sheets

General

If down low on beach add a plastic sheet under camera to protect from sand.

Use manual focus if difficult for auto to focus for example if it's windy or the light is low.
Take a plastic bag or purpose made sleeve, to put camera and gear in if it rains.

Hat, insect repellent, sunscreen, water, raincoat, jacket or long sleeved top and light full pants. (often at sunset and sunrise mosquitoes are bad).

Camera, cards, batteries, money and phone.

Clean your camera lens and take a microfibre cloth

Tripod.

Think Safety First - often we get carried away trying to get that unique angle, always think SAFETY first.
Check the weather forecast before you leave and tell someone where you are going.

Golden hour and blue hour are the best times to go out, so go early in the morning or later in the afternoon to ensure the best light.
When you arrive on scene:

Think about what story you want to tell.

How would it look close up, how would it look low, high, different angles, horizontal or vertical?

Try to create the feeling of the image as you want it, lonely and isolated or welcoming and peaceful. Etc.

Use grey card to get right white balance.

Check your camera settings, is the ISO on 100, are you in the right setting, if you are shooting in RAW is it turned on.

Check out where the light is coming from, where are the shadows falling, how much difference is there between the light and dark areas of the image. Often it works best if the light is off to the side.

Walk around looking for what you want to be the main object that your image is about.

Look for foreground interest.

Take a few test shots and look at them in the camera, are their any distractions, are is the image looking the way you want.

Can you create a leading line?

Can you place the main object on one of the third lines or sweet spots of the composition rules.

Are there complementary colors, patterns of textures to add interest and depth.

Use a fairly large depth of field, f12 to f32 or whatever your camera goes up to.

Check if you have IS (image stability) on your camera or lens. If it does not have a tripod mode then turn it off.

Take a wide angle image and then see how many other photos you can find within the image.

Simplify.

As you take your camera off the tripod, turn the IS back on:)

Landscape photography sky
Great tutorial (funny too)
            http://www.lightstalking.com/sky

www.ingramcontent.com/pod-product-compliance
Lightning Source LLC
Chambersburg PA
CBHW040926180526
45159CB00002BA/625